PROJECT MANAGEMENT LAYMAN'S GUIDE

A Concise Study of the Seventh Edition

PHILL AKINWALE, OPM3, PMP, PMI-ACP

Praizi⬤nMed🏃a
Real World Project Management Training Solutions

Project Management Essentials published by Praizion Media

P.O Box 22241, Mesa, AZ 85277

E-mail: info@praizion.com

www.praizion.com

Author

Phillip Akinwale, MSc, OPM3, PMP, PMI-ACP, CAPM, PSM, CSM

ISBN 978-1-934579-93-0

9 781934 579930

CONTENTS

CHAPTER ONE

INTRODUCTION

The *PMBOK® Guide* Seventh Edition is a whole new configuration compared to previous editions. In the seventh edition, you only find one reference of process groups that have been in existence for decades and that is on page 170

and 171.

The dominance of process groups as it was in previous editions is not reflected in the seventh.

As for the knowledge areas, you will not find the knowledge areas in this book. Instead, what you find is a mishmash of "knowledge areas on process groups", which is now called domains. This is a different set of domains from anything PMI has used in the past. The language used to describe the domains is however very knowledge-area centric.

So, you have domains, but you don't have knowledge areas and you have a tiny little mention of process groups on page 170 and 171.

Let's jump into the seventh edition with a super-fast review!

Chapter 1 is an introduction to the standard. The key definitions we had in the sixth edition of projects, project management, programs PMOs, has been whittled down to just two pages. Let's review a quick summary of these key definitions.

Summary of key definitions

- Outcome: The end result of a project including its value and benefits.
- Portfolio: A collection of projects, programs, sub portfolios and operations managed collectively to achieve the organization's strategic objectives.

- Product: A quantifiable artifact that could be an end-item or sub-item.

- Program: A collection of 2 or more interrelated projects, subprograms and program activities.
- Project: A temporary endeavor executed to create a unique deliverable.
- Project management: the application of leadership, knowledge, skills, tools and techniques to a project, to deliver a desired outcome of benefits and value for the customer and stakeholders.
- Project manager: The individual assigned to lead the project team and coordinate the effective management of the project.
- Project team: The people assigned to perform the project work
- System for value delivery: A system for delivering value to stakeholders through associated portfolios, programs, projects and operational work.

- Value: The net quantifiable benefits experienced by a customer. Also the worth, importance or usefulness of a deliverable.

CHAPTER TWO

SYSTEM FOR VALUE DELIVERY

Chapter 2 describes a new term. It is called "a system for value delivery".

The summary of the *system for value delivery* is

that it aims to deliver desired outcomes to stakeholders.

The focus is not on the output (or deliverables) alone. It is more on the outcome.

When you take a look at a *value delivery system*, it consists of things you may be familiar with, projects, programs, portfolios and operations. These components make up the system for value delivery.

Through the system for value delivery, outcomes are provided. The components in a value delivery system create deliverables which are used to produce desired outcomes of value, benefits and satisfaction for the customer.

An outcome is the end-result or consequence of

a process or a product.

Focusing on outcomes, choices and decisions emphasizes the long-range performance of the project. The outcomes create benefits, which are gains realized by the organization.

Benefits in turn create value, which is something of worth importance or usefulness.

This value delivery system exists within a company or organization, which could be seen as the internal environment. beyond that also exists an external environment such as a state, region, country or continent.

So, in summary, we're looking for a favorable outcome, which also means benefits and value in desired describable or quantifiable amounts.

Before every project starts, there should be an idea of the value and benefits to be realized in specific terms. This could evolve as the project progresses.

See this as a formal term for related portfolios, programs, projects, and operations. Whether they are several projects in a program or whether they are projects standing alone in a portfolio. The idea is they are all working together to create that outcome to deliver benefits and value.

Related information (from all value delivery components) flows across the system.

The information flow is from senior leadership to portfolios, down to programs and to operations and back. This information describes results and outcomes for concerned stakeholders.

Governance

In this second chapter, mention is made of governance, which is the framework within which authority is exercised. With governance, there are rules, guidelines, and chains of authority to follow. Without governance there could be chaos in a value delivery system.

Functions associated with projects

There are various roles associated with projects. This relates to the leading and management of work. These responsibilities include:

- Provide oversight and coordination

- Present objectives and feedback

- Facilitate and support

- Perform work and contribute insights

- Apply expertise

- Provide business direction and insight

- Provide resources and direction

- Maintain governance

The project environment

Now this is a big change from the sixth edition where you had enterprise environmental factors (EEFs) and organizational process assets (OPAs).

Instead in the seventh edition, it simply reads internal environment and external environment.

The internal environment consists of internal EEFs, and it also combines that with OPAs. Examples include; governance documentation, data assets, knowledge assets, organizational culture structure and governance.

The external environment refers to, marketplace conditions, social and cultural factors, regulatory clauses, commercial databases, academic research, industry standards and financial considerations such as exchange rates. You don't have any hold over those. That's why they're external. This includes the physical environment itself, and acts of God, including weather and things like that.

Product management

In this edition, the writers have elevated product management and it's good because product management has become a bit of a buzzword in today's business world.

The word product is very noticeable in agile. When we talk about Agile, we often talk about value in a *product*. So, it's important to understand what a product is and its cycle of life

Now a lot of times in Agile what we work on is not necessarily called a project, we could say we're working on an endeavor to add value to an existing product and that should compound benefits and good outcomes the customer experiences.

A product could be described as an artifact that is being produced. It's quantifiable and can either be an item in itself or a component item.

Product lifecycle

Every product has a lifecycle.

1. Introduction: This is the introduction of a product from the very first project. It is produced and introduced in a firm, maybe

as part of a program. This could be part of a multi-year program.

2. Growth: As we evolve through the program, a second project could be authorized and executed to add more features. That's the growth of the product. The product grows with more additions.

3. Maturity: Ultimately, we get into the maturity of the product. We have revision upon revision, to keep the product benefits and value flowing with good outcomes.

4. Retirement: Ultimately, we get into the decline and retirement of the product.

In summary, we could have several projects to enhance a product. It started off with one project to get the product launched and into production and then several successive projects to add value to the first increment.

After running its course, the product benefits ultimately decline and the product is retired. So that's introduction growth, maturity and then decline, and that pretty much closes out the first part of the seventh edition.

A quote says, "It is not the strongest of the species that survives, it's the species that can adapt to change." And that makes a case for change management. When we adapt to change, we have staying power! Changing with the times is vital. Just ask Blockbuster, Kodak or Toys R Us. They'll tell you!

CHAPTER THREE

PROJECT MANAGEMENT PRINCIPLES

Moving on to **Chapter 3**, we will study the new 12 project management principles.

The principles are listed without any specific

weighting or order, and they have a lot of overlap with general management principles. In fact, if you work for any progressive company in today's modern world, they typically have some bearing of principles or moral compass. That's what this is very, very similar to.

These principles are founded on the four values (responsibility, respect, fairness and honesty) from the PMI Code of Ethics and Professional Conduct. Let's cover these principles one by one.

Principle 1

Be a diligent respectful and caring steward

- You've likely heard this at one point or another, where you need to respect those resources that have been entrusted to you?

- This could be physical resources, team members, equipment, materials and supplies.

- Stewards act responsibly. They carry out activities with integrity, care and trustworthiness. They're not dishonest and they also are aware of compliance, whether it is internal or external guidelines. A good steward demonstrates a broad commitment to financial impacts, social impacts and environmental impacts. So, be trustworthy, show integrity, show care and compliance, and that's really it!

Principle 2
Create A Collaborative Project Team Environment

My mentor and coach in leadership John C. Maxwell, says "teamwork makes a dreamwork" and it's true! Without the team where would you be?

Another quote from Anna Wintour, editor-in-chief of Vogue, "You are nothing without the team." It's true! When you think about it, projects are delivered by project teams not a lone project manager or rock-star!

When we think about the team, we should focus

on structures, procedures and, process that help the team thrive, see? We want to create a collaborative environment. We want to focus on individual learning, team learning, alignment with organizational cultures and guidelines, and we want to optimize the team's contribution.

So, the general idea is project teams are made up of humans, right? Individuals who have diverse skills. We often use the term T-shaped skills.

Now, where you put humans together, you need structures such as team agreements, organizational guidelines, structure, and processes. We also need to be very clear on authority. The condition of having the right (within a given context), to make relevant decisions.

When a team is formed, clarification should be made regarding accountability, and who is ultimately answerable for a task or deliverable.

Clasification should also be made regarding responsibility (the condition of being obligated to do or fulfill something).

When we think about teams, fostering a diverse project team can enrich the project environment by bringing together different perspectives.

In fact, research shows that the more diverse a team is, the better the outcome!

Principle 3

Effectively Engage with Stakeholders

A stakeholder is someone who could influence a project or someone who the project could affect.

A stakeholder could also be someone who thinks the project will impact them. So, our job as project personnel, is to engage stakeholders in a proactive manner, to engage stakeholders to the degree needed and to contribute to project success and customer satisfaction through that engagement.

If you engage stakeholders proactively, they will

be where you want them to be at the right time, and contribute to project success.

Stakeholders are powerful. They can make or break a project. When it comes to scope, schedule, cost, the project team, planning outcomes, culture, realizing benefits, managing risk, quality and success, stakeholders are right there in the center.

That's why we need to proactively engage stakeholders. A lot of times people forget the project team. Those individuals are also stakeholders. The team, that's a group of your stakeholders as well! Customers, a governing body in charge of a particular regulation are also stakeholders.

Effective engagement means knowing what

matters most to stakeholders and attending to those concerns to get the most robust outcome possible.

Principle 4

Focus on Value

Continually evaluate and adjust the project by aligning it to business objectives and intended benefits and value. Value is the ultimate indicator of project success so focus on real needs!

Business needs should be connected to a business case and a benefits management strategy also comes into this discussion.

The reason for which the project and all associated needs are provided should be related to strategy.

The reason why we get this funding for project X is because project X is going to help us meet our strategic business objectives.

Principle 5

Recognize, evaluate and respond to system interactions

What does this principle about system interactions mean? In this principle, our focus is on systems thinking. This involves seeing the big picture of how systems interact.

What is a system? A set of interacting and independent components that function as a unified whole.

A project is a system of several interconnected components, but it's within a wider system of a company. Think about the company, it's within a wider system of a business environment or a marketplace.

When you take a look at the marketplace, see it as a system within a bigger system of a country or region or state.

When you recognize systems interacting, you are employing "systems thinking", and you're seeing how the project team interacts within the project and, you're seeing the project adds value to the firm. In addition to that, you see how the firm adds value to the world. That's how you should see systems.

This principle involves recognizing, evaluating

and responding to systems interactions that lead to positive outcomes.

Principle 6

Demonstrate and adapt leadership behaviors

What are some of the leadership behaviors we should see in a leader? How about starting with trustworthiness? Being a trustworthy person, being someone who can articulate vision, someone who can cast vision, someone who can help those who lack understanding see the vision!

A leader should have the ability and drive to seek resources where there are none. Someone who has the courage to challenge the status quo, someone who has self-awareness, who can show empathy! A leader also understands the importance of being likable. Someone who has paid their dues in the firm by adding tremendous value through projects and programs that they've been part of, being a role model for desired behavior.

That is what leadership is all about in this context.

Being a servant leader is critical for project managers and that's why anyone taking the professional project management exams these days should absolutely be tuned in to serve in leadership!

Principle 7

Tailor Based on Context

Design the project development approach based on the context of the project, its objectives, stakeholders, governance and the environment.

Use just enough process to achieve the desired outcome while maximizing value, managing cost and enhancing speed.

Now when I go to companies to train, a lot of times, they would see the massive *PMBOK®* *Guide*. It's big! Hundreds of pages. 756 pages at the time!

When they saw this book, the first question they would ask is "Phill, are you bringing us more work to do? We already have enough!" And I tell them no. I'm going to simplify it for you. I'm going to show you how to tailor using the 80-20 principle or the 80-20 rule.

You've got all of these processes you could use, 49 of them. Just remember, 20% of the processes will give you an 80% payoff or an 80% return (whatever that may be on your project), that's the idea.

So together with the project management office and taking governance into account, project teams should decide on the best approach for their projects and that's tailoring.

Tailoring factors in these questions:

- What tool should we use?
- Which resources do we use?
- What are the documents that we are obligated to use?
- What methods?
- What practices?
- Do we need to do any experimentation?
- What kind of project are we working on right now?
- Are we working on a Predictive, a Hybrid or an Agile project?

These are some of the questions you should take into consideration. Based on the answers, tailor the project to use the bare minimum processes, tools, resources and methods.

Principle 8

Build Quality into Processes and Deliverables

Quality simply put is fitness for use, conformance to requirements and customer satisfaction.

As the principle states, build quality into processes and deliverables. It's a no-brainer! Why wouldn't you build quality in?

As you're building quality in, remember it has several dimensions such as quality of performance, the quality in the deliverable, and functioning at the required performance level!

We expect conformity, reliability and resilience.

Does it hold up under tension or unforeseen failures?

Satisfaction, uniformity, efficiency, sustainability are also quality-related terms.

Principle 9
Navigate Complexity

Complexity is a characteristic of a project or other endeavor that is difficult to manage or predict due to system behavior, ambiguity and human behavior.

Look at these as sources of complexity.

1) human behavior.

2) system behavior.

3) uncertainty and ambiguity.

4) technological innovation.

So when you say complex, complexity may emerge and impact the project in any area at any point.

Do know that complexity many a time is not perceived at first? But as you proceed through the project, the complexity begins to emerge!

You can't predict human behavior. System behavior may also be hard to predict, because we have emergence in systems where a totally unexpected response results from adding or changing parts of the system!

So when we talk about complexity, be aware that it is a characteristic that has different variables contributing to it. Complexity is also subject to various interpretations depending on who is involved.

Breaking work down into smaller components in iterations enables the team deal with complexity better.

Principle 10

Optimize Risk Responses

Whatever you do, choose the best response for identified risks. So, you must continually evaluate your risk exposure and take the best course of action to maximize positive impacts and minimize negative impacts.

There are different ways we can respond to risks. We can "A-TEAM" or we can "EASEE".

What do I mean by that? It's a mnemonic A-T-E-A-M.

- Avoid – avoid the risk
- Transfer – transfer the risk to someone else
- Escalate – escalate risks to higher authority
- Accept – do nothing proactively
- Mitigate – reduce the probability or impact

What do I mean by EASEE? E-A-S-E-E? It is a mnemonic for the following:

- Escalate – escalate to a higher authority
- Accept – do nothing proactively
- Share – share with another entity
- Exploit – make the risk 100% certain
- Enhance – increase the probability/impact

So, whether you are dealing with negative risks (threats) OR positive risks (opportunities), choose the best risk response and optimize your responses for the customer's advantage.

Principle 11

Embrace adaptability and resiliency

Build adaptability and resiliency into the organizations and project team's approaches to help the project accommodate change and recover from setbacks.

Building adaptability and resiliency in will help advance the work of the project in the face of obstacles and adversity.

I used to work in a bank Salomon Smith Barney.

When part of Salomon and Citigroup decided to merge, we had a backup trade floor just in case something went wrong with one of our trade floors at a different location. This was a way of building in redundancy as a coping mechanism with resiliency. The ability to absorb any shock, to bounce back, continue business as usual.

There are also instances where you need to build this resiliency into a product or into a team, and that's why we have professionals who know the best way to build resiliency into a team.

It goes beyond just thinking about contingencies. You've got to think further than that. You got to build resiliency into the process! Build it into the very fabric of the organization.

When we engage diverse teams, employ short

feedback loops, continuous learn and prototype, we are building in resiliency and adaptability!

Having open conversations to enable news travel quicker than normal also helps us be adaptable and stay ahead.

Other examples of building in resiliency and adaptability includes, deferring decision-making to the last responsible moment, having leaders who are supportive of the project and team.

Open-ended design that balances speed and stability is another coping mechanism to enable resiliency and adaptability.

Unexpected changes and circumstances in a project system can also present opportunities to optimize value delivery. Project teams should use problem-solving in a holistic thinking approach, and employ systems thinking to tackle changes and unplanned events.

So, building adaptability and resiliency into a project keeps project teams focused on the delivering desired outcomes. I call it "bounceback-ability". You want to have that because change will happen!

Principle 12

Enable change to achieve the

envisioned future state

The summary of this principle is this, *be a change agent.* Enabling change in the organization could be a challenge.

People may seem inherently resistant to change, but perhaps if we are change agents and catalysts, if we can prepare our team members and the organization better, perhaps things will go a lot smoother.

It's also important to adapt the speed of change to the change appetite of stakeholders and the firm at large.

Also adapt the change to the cost and ability of stakeholders. Too much change in a short time can lead to resistance. It could also lead to change fatigue, so we need to be careful and ensure we are changing at the right time in the right amounts, see?

Remaining relevant in today's business world is a fundamental challenge of all organizations and relevance entails being responsive to stakeholder needs and desires through effective change management.

PART 2

CHAPTER FOUR

PERFORMANCE DOMAINS

Let's move on to part 2 of the seventh edition.

As I said in the first chapter, domains are a combination of knowledge areas and process groups! If you ever studied them, this will be easy to understand.

The language is very knowledge area-driven.

Here are the domains:
1) Stakeholders
2) Team
3) Development Approach And Life Cycle
4) Planning
5) Project Work
6) Delivery
7) Measurement
8) Uncertainty.

This is really process groups and knowledge areas combined! Stakeholders team, project work delivery, measurement and uncertainty, we could map those directly back to chapters from the knowledge areas of old. So, don't feel this is entirely new and you're starting off from scratch.

There's a lot that you already know.

DOMAIN 1
STAKEHOLDER

This domain addresses activities and functions associated with stakeholders.

We need to think about identifying our stakeholders, understanding them and analyzing their power and interest levels. As project personnel, we should be involved in prioritizing our stakeholder focus and engaging our stakeholders. We should also monitor our stakeholder performance to ensure we're doing a good job with our stakeholder all-round. We should also validate our results.

The outcome you would expect from a successful stakeholder domain execution is, a productive working relationship with stakeholders, stakeholder agreement with project objectives, and stakeholders (who are project beneficiaries) are supportive and satisfied.

And that is pretty much it for stakeholders.

DOMAIN 2
TEAM

The team performance domain addresses activities and functions associated with the people who are responsible for producing project deliverables (which realize business outcomes).

The following definitions are relevant to the team performance domain: the project manager, the project management team and the project team.

Project manager: This is the induvial assigned to lead the project and all concerned parties.

Project management team: The project management team are members of the project team who are directly involved in project management activities. On a project team, you have some people doing the actual *project management* work and those are in the project management team.

Project team: A set of individuals performing the actual work of the project. These are people doing actual development work. For example, writing code, building a structure, creating a produc or delivering a service.

Now this distinction had been around for quite a while. In the world of Agile, we don't care about such. We just say team! And team is team and that's it!

Now moving on here, a few topics to be aware of, in this domain:

- Project management is all about applying knowledge, skills, tools and techniques for management activities.

- On every project, there are leadership activities. There is a concept of centralized management and leadership around one individual (project manager) but there's also distributed management and leadership (around the entire team, where each person carries out project management and leadership functions).

Decentralized leadership is taking away the project manager focus to a team focus for leadership and management.

Instead of relying on one person to make a decision, anyone on the team can facilitate that!

Leadership in the context of a team, could refer to servant leadership.

Things servant leaders, do includes: they remove obstacles, they are diversion shields, they encourage development of opportunities, they cast vision and they guide the team and grow the team.

Each team has its unique culture developed by its members. While developing an effective culture, consideration should be made of transparency. Upholding, integrity, respect and positive discourse are good traits for any team culture.

Team members should be supportive of each other, courageous to do the right thing and ready to celebrate success.

High-performing teams are open in their communication. They should have a shared understanding and a shared ownership of whatever they are involved with.

Trust, collaboration, adaptability, resilience, empowerment and recognition are great traits for teams to espouse.

Leadership skills such as vision, critical, thinking and motivation, are key skills for team-members and should not just be relegated to a project manager. Everyone on the team should have these skills.

Aspirational standards for emotional intelligence (EI), decision-making, being able to resolve conflict; and communication guidelines could be documented in a team charter.

When it comes to resolving conflict, having a definition of what done is, and a definition of what ready is, should also be documented in the team charter.

It is also important that a project manager or a servant leader, tailor their leadership style based on the experience and maturity of the team, organizational governance structures, and distributed project teams.

The way you lead a team that is geographically dispersed could be very different.

DOMAIN 3

DEVELOPMENT APPROACH AND LIFECYCLE

In the development approach and life cycle performance domain we address the concepts of choosing the best development approach and life cycle.

It starts with understanding the deliverable and then deciding on the development approach. In addition to this, one should also consider the concept of cadence.

If you're using Kanban versus Scrum, you're going to have different cadences of course, right?

Kanban is not cadence-driven but Scrum is. Scrum sprints are to be a specific cadence, a specific rhythm. We could have two weeks sprints, three weeks sprints, four weeks sprints, one-week sprint or less, it really depends.

We consider these aspects in the development approach and life cycle performance domain.

Depending on how predictive, hybridized or agile we are, there are number of possibilities.

DOMAIN 4
PLANNING

If you fail to plan you plan to fail. So, plan everything plannable! Plan the development approach. Plan how deliverables will be delivered, plan based on market conditions.

A big part of planning is estimating. You're going to have to estimate schedule. You must estimate cost and understand if there's any management reserves.

Management reserves are not part of the cost baseline or the project budget. These are for unexpected scope and unknowns.

Within the project budget, we do have the cost baseline and contingency reserves.

Project teams should also plan communications, resources, procurements, changes, metrics alignment and many other variables.

DOMAIN 5
PROJECT WORK

The project work performance domain addresses activities and functions associated with establishing project processes, managing physical resources and fostering a learning environment.

Key things to think about here are balancing, competing, constraints, maintaining team focus, project communications and engagement, managing physical resources, working with procurements and getting things done.

This domain is also concerned with monitoring the intake of new work as a result of enterprise environmental factors. It also involves learning throughout the project, harnessing knowledge management, (through tacit knowledge and explicit knowledge).

This domain includes ensuring efficient (least effort) and effective (successful) project performance. It involves efficient management of physical resources, AND effective handling of change to mention a few.

DOMAIN 6

DELIVERY

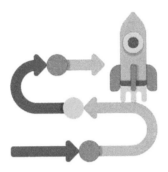

This addresses activities and functions associated with delivering the scope and quality that the project was undertaken to achieve.

Here we talk about the definition of done, scope, requirements, quality and the cost of quality.

Our goal is to deliver value and while delivering value, of course, we are going to uphold quality because delivery is not just about scope, quality is a very important aspect as well.

We should also factor in internal failure costs, external failure costs, prevention costs, appraisal costs and understand the cost of quality (costs of upholding quality for the life of the produt).

Also be aware that suboptimal outcomes happen. The question is; *"What will you do when they happen?"*

You should learn from your suboptimal (less than ideal) outcomes, and continue to improve. Try again until you succeed! There might be several rounds before you actually get a desired outcome, whatever it is.

Projects require deliberate investment in sometimes uncertain outcomes. Sometimes you're working on a new medicine, a new compound, something that you've never done before. In such cases, suboptimal outcomes are expected until we get to that perfect one that we can release.

DOMAIN 7
MEASUREMENT

The measurement performance domain addresses activities and functions associated with assessing project performance and taking appropriate actions to maintain acceptable performance.

Firstly, you want to establish effective measures. You want to ask the question; "What should we be measuring?"

Whenever in doubt about what to measure, use the five whys! Ask the questions:

- Why do you want that metric?
    - Because I want to check team performance.
- Why do you want to check on team performance?
    - Because I want to make sure the project gets done on time.

And you can ask why five times, and a lot of times, you get down to a metric and a reason where you can help better direct and mold the specific measurements and even key performance indicators (KPIs) being used.

Sometimes it's a wrong KPI. Now when we talk about KPIs, we have leading indicators that show us things as they're happening and we have lagging indicators, which reveal details about what happened after the fact, as it were in reflection of why something happened. So always ask why stakeholders want a specific metric and get down to the bottom of it.

Effective metrics must be SMART, (specific, meaningful, achievable, relevant and timely).

What should we measure? This could include:

- Deliverable metrics
- Delivery
- Baseline performance
- Resources
- Business value
- Stakeholder engagement and happiness
- Forecasts

What we measure depends on the specific project and stakeholder interests. We could measure a variety of things from earned value (reporting on schedule and cost performance) to net promotor score to see how readily our stakeholders would promote us to others.

We could use a mood chart to understand the emotional state of our stakeholders.

We could use traffic lights and dashboards, but the question is what do we need?

Do we need an information radiator to rapidly share the information?

Do we need visual controls, such as burn down charts and burn up charts if we're in a more Agile environment?

It really boils down to the project, and we know

we are successful in this area when we have a reliable understanding of the status of the project, actionable data to facilitate decision-making and timely and appropriate actions to keep project performance on track.

DOMAIN 8

UNCERTAINTY

The final performance domain is the uncertainty performance domain. Uncertainty can be described as a lack of understanding and awareness of issues, events, path to follow or solutions to pursue. Consequently, it is tied very closely to the topic of risk.

What is risk after all? It's an uncertain event or condition that if it occurs has a positive or negative effect on one or more project objectives. My buddy, the risk doctor says "Risk is uncertainty that matters to your project."

So how do we manage uncertainty? Uncertainty can be managed by first gathering information and preparing for multiple outcomes.

We can also manage uncertainty by building in resilience. Bear in mind that multiple designs or alternatives can be investigated early in the project as a way of reducing uncertainty.

We also manage uncertain events by progressive elaboration (iterative and frequent planning), experiments, prototyping, reframing.

Reframing

Reframing includes the following:

- Diversity: We use the concept of diversity by looking at things from different perspectives.
- Balance: balancing the type of data used. Instead of just using forecasting data. We can also use data that is a lagging indicator. Use leading and lagging indicators.

We could also use the process of fail-safe mechanisms, the process of iterations, all of these are ways we can deal with uncertainty.

Volatility

Volatility (rapid and unpredictable change) exists within certain projects. Projects could address volatility through alternatives analysis, finding and evaluating alternatives and putting aside some sort of reserve.

Risk

Last but not least, we have the topic of risk.

To effectively manage risks, first plan how to manage the risks, identify the risks and then analyze the risks qualitatively at a minimum. In some instances, quantitative risks analysis is required. Next, you should plan how to respond to the risks (both positive and negative).

When we discussed, the principles I talked about the mnemonics (A-TEAM) and (EASEE) which you could use to recall responses.

Let's have a quick refresh!

- ATEAM: If you're dealing with threats, you can (A-TEAM) avoid, transfer, escalate, accept or mitigate.

- EASEE: If you're dealing with opportunities, you can exploit, escalate, share, enhance or accept.

Finally, teams should implement the decided-upon risk responses and monitor risks throughout the project. New risks should also be logged and if risks have changed, the risk register should be updated.

Success in this domain is evident when there is an awareness of the environment in which projects occur, including but not limited to, the technical, social, political market and economic environments.

CHAPTER FIVE

TAILORING

et's move on to learn about tailoring. There are several tools, processes and methods one can use on a project, but the team should tailor these options for each project. Tailor project management options to your unique circumstance.

Projects exist in diverse environments that could have an influence on them. Prior to tailoring the project, its environment needs to be analyzed and understood.

Steps in tailoring include:

1. **Selecting a development and delivery approach.**
   - Is the organization or project best suited for predictive, hybrid or agile?
2. **Tailoring it for the organization.**
   - some organizations may have an overarching project approach, project methodology or developmental process. Based on the unique

situation, teams may have to tailor the project approach end artifacts to this.

3. **Tailoring it for the project.**

   - Tailoring for the project entails considering the deliverable being produced, the team size, geography, experience, access to customer, culture, buying, trust and empowerment.

4. **Implement its ongoing improvement.**

   - Because tailoring is not a one-time event, the team should be prepared to be engaged with improvements go forward.

CHAPTER SIX

MODELS, METHODS AND ARTIFACTS

Let's review the topic of models, methods and artifacts.

Model: A model is a thinking strategy to explain a process, framework or phenomenon.

Method: A method is the means for achieving an outcome.

Artifact: An artifact is simply put a template, document or project deliverable.

Chapter 4 of the *PMBOK® Guide* Seventh Edition explores lots of these models, methods and artifacts, but that is beyond the scope of this quick review. I will give you a few high-level ideas about models, methods and artifacts.

Models Summary

Some of my favorite models include: the Situational Leadership Model, the hygiene and motivation factors from Herzberg, theory X, theory Y and theory Z. John Kotter's 8-step process for leading. The Stacey Matrix also known as the Stacey model, Tuckman's ladder and the Thomas-Kilmann conflict mode instrument.

Methods Summary

Examples of models include; alternatives analysis, earned value management, expected monetary value, probability and impact matrix, and sensitivity analysis to mention a few.

Artifacts Summary

Examples of artifacts are business case, project charter, roadmap, risk register and release plan.

Conclusion

And that concludes our review of the PMBOK Guide7th Edition. I hope you found this review to be succinct and helpful. I wish you all the very best whatever you're doing, whether you are taking the PMP® exam, CAPM® exam or anything else you do with project management.

CHAPTER SEVEN
Final Project
Management Quiz

1. Project examples could include which of the following?
A. Publication of a children's book
B. Covid-19 vaccine
C. Human beings landing on the moon
D. All of the above

2. The *PMBOK® Guide* and the Standard for Project Management are both in one book.
A. True
B. False

3. A _____ is a temporary endeavor undertaken to create a unique product, service, or result.

A. Project

B. Operation

C. Program

D. Portfolio

4. Fulfillment of project objectives may produce which of the following?

A. A product that is not unique and can be either a component of another item

B. A non-unique service or a capability to perform a service

C. A unique result, such as an outcome or document

D. A repetitive task to add value to produce a repeat product or service

5. Examples of projects include which of the following?

A. Expanding a tour guide service and merging two organizations

B. Improving a business process within an organization

C. Acquiring a hardware system and exploring for oil in a region

D. All of the options

6. Projects, programs, subsidiary portfolios, and operations managed as a group to achieve strategic objectives. What does this describe?

A. Project

B. Operation

C. Program

D. Portfolio

7. _____ is concerned with the ongoing production of goods and/or services. It ensures that business operations continue

efficiently by using the optimal resources needed to meet customer demands.

A. Project management
B. Operations management
C. Program management
D. Portfolio management

8. What is a document established by an authority, custom, or general consent as a model or example known as?

A. Standard
B. Regulation
C. Legal Restriction
D. Governmental agency rule

9. Which of the following moves an organization from one state to another?

A. Project
B. Process
C. Procedure
D. Benefit

10.   The benefit that the results of a
specific project provide to its stakeholders
is known as _____

A. Business value
B. Benefits management
C. Stockholder equity
D. Strategic alignment

11.   An agile approach to planning_____.
A. Results in plans that encourage change and
that are easily changed
B. Focuses on the plan documents rather than
the planning process
C. Results in a fully defined schedule and
budget
D. Fully defines product features early in the
project

12.   Agile is best used when _____
A. There is low variability is needed on the
project
B. Change is unlikely and static requirements
are needed
C. Experimentation and discovery are needed
for the solution

D. Little chance of change and high certainty

13. Which of the following is most important on all projects?
- *Deliver on Time*
- *Deliver on Budget*
- *Deliver all Planned Scope*
- *Meet Customer Needs*
- *Meet Quality Requirements*
- *Team Satisfaction*

A. Time
B. Budget
C. The 3 lower-level items on the list
D. The 3 higher level items on the list

14. Which of these is NOT a function associated with a project?
A. Provide oversight and coordination
B. Present objectives and feedback
C. Control the company revenues
D. Perform work and contribute insights

15. External environments include:
   A. Infrastructure
   B. Academic research
   C. Information technology software
   D. Resource availability and commercial databases

16. The PMI® Code of Ethics includes _____ (select all that apply)
   A. Responsibility and Respect
   B. Respect and Bureaucracy
   C. Resiliency and Responsibility
   D. Fairness and Respect

17. The first principle about stewardship includes:
   A. Integrity and Rewards
   B. Care and Remuneration
   C. Trustworthiness and Compliance
   D. All of the options

18.   The second principle encourages a

_____

   team environment.

A. Communicative
B. Collaborative
C. Participative
D. Conniving

19.   Stakeholder engagement is
   _____ for success

A. A bit important
B. Not important
C. Critical
D. Subjective

20.   According to PMI, value is _____
   and driver of projects.

A. The ultimate success indicator
B. The monetary indicator
C. Tangible
D. Quantifiable

21.   According to PMI:

A. A project is a system
B. Systems occasionally change
C. A project is not a system
D. Systems thinking is a partial view

22.   Which of these terms best describes leadership?

A. Authority
B. Position
C. Title
D. Influence

23.   According to PMI, tailoring is

_____

A. Iterative
B. Continuous
C. A constant process
D. All of the above

24.   According to PMI, quality involves

_____

A. Aggravating stakeholders
B. Meeting acceptance criteria

C. Ensuring project processes are inappropriate

D. All of the options

25.   According to PMI, complexity is the result of _____

A. Human behavior

B. System interactions

C. Uncertainty and ambiguity

D. All of the options

26.   Project risk management should be _____

A. Appropriate to the significance of the risk

B. Cost effective in meeting personal goals and targets

C. Realistic within the operations context

D. Disagreed upon by all parties

27.   Resiliency is best described as the _____

A. Ability to respond to change

B. Ability to absorb impacts/recover

C. Ability to configure a project

D. Ability to focus on project outcomes

28.   According to PMI, too much change

_____

A. Could lead to over-energizing the team
B. Could lead to change fatigue and resistance
C. Could help enable stakeholder engagement
D. Is not possible because change always contributes

29.   You are working on a project with low requirements uncertainty and a low technical uncertainty. Due to these low levels of uncertainty, which model should you select?

A. Hybrid
B. Agile
C. Iterative
D. Predictive

30.   Which of the following factors typically does not influence the nature of project delivery method selected?

A. Deliverable
B. Organization
C. Project

D. Motivation and machines

31.   Which of the following is not typically a life-cycle

phase?

A. Feasibility, Design
B. Build, Test
C. Deploy, Close
D. Monitoring and Controlling

32.   Metrics on a project should not be planned until the executing stage.

A. True
B. False

33.   Values clustered around a desired value with little scatter. What does this describe?

A. Highly Accurate and Highly Precise
B. Accuracy is low
C. Precision is high
D. Defective

34.   In agile, the Scrum Master is solely accountable

for ensuring project process conferment.
   A. True
   B. False

35.   The best approach for delivery in Kanban is:
A. Every 2 weeks
B. Every 4 weeks
C. When it makes sense to do so
D. At the specific order of the flow master

36.   Which of the following is NOT a legit artifact of agile?
A. Burn up chart
B. Burn down chart
C. Risk baseline
D. Sprint backlog

37.   Which of the following is NOT a risk?
A. Resource X has been called off the project
B. Resource Y may not be available

C. Resource Z a key resource may be called off the project

D. The build has a reputation for being unstable

38. You are managing a project. One of your team members has an opportunity to move onto another project that would be an incredible opportunity for them. Your project is critical and you know with one phone call, you could prevent this person from leaving your team. What should you do?

A. Do nothing

B. Make the call so as not to lose this valuable resource

C. Support your team member's access to opportunity

D. Offer up another team member that is not as valuable to your team

39. You are managing a construction project. You have received quotes from three different suppliers and are currently evaluating the proposals. After work one

evening, you just happened to bump into one of the suppliers at your favorite hang-out. After a few minutes of casual conversation, he makes the statement that if his company is chosen as the supplier that he will personally see that you get financially compensated. What should you do?

A. Ask how much you would be compensated
B. Politely excuse yourself from this conversation because stewards behave honestly and ethically
C. Take him up on the offer because no one will ever know
D. Postpone your answer until you talk with your lawyer friend

40.   You become aware that the FAA is planning to change the flight paths for a major airport located just two miles from your nuclear plant. The new fight path would reduce airline noise for local residents but would require more than 50% of the air traffic to fly directly over the cooling towers. What should you do?

A.   Seek appropriate counsel and guidance

B.   Do nothing

C.   Support the FAA plans for change

D.   Contact the FAA and partition for the

change not to occur

41.   You have just been assigned to a new project. Both you as well as all of your team members are very experienced but have never worked together on the same project before. What is the first thing you should do?

A. Create a Project Charter
B. Document the requirements for the project
C. Pick a suitable collaboration software for your team
D. Develop a Team Agreement

42.   You have been assigned to manage a project with many team members. You know that an organizational structure will help coordinate the effort associated with the project work. You know these structures can be based upon a number of

factors. You want to develop an organization structure for your project, which of the following is NOT an approach you could use?

A. By Role
B. By Function
C. By Experience
D. By Authority

43. You know that a diverse project team can enrich the project environment by bringing together different perspectives. You are at a point in the project where you need to bring on additional resources. Your current team is comprised of organizational staff. Since you are wanting to bring in a fresh perspective, which option would you not choose to bring on?

A. Contracted Contributors
B. Organizational Staff
C. Volunteers
D. External Third Parties

44.   Engaging with stakeholders is time-intensive during project planning. The sponsor would like to know what all the fuss is about and get an explanation from you as the project manager about what is taking so long. How would you explain the why the time is needed?

A. To effectively engage stakeholders in project decisions and execution based on the analysis of their needs, interests, and potential impact

B. To ensure the stakeholders are receiving the reports in the format they would like

C. To effectively place the right people in the correct role to support achieving the project objectives on time and within budget

D. To be able to document which stakeholder is unaware, neutral, leading, or supportive

45.   You are relatively new to Project Management. You want to do a little research or studying of the topic Stakeholder Engagement. Which course should you take?

A. Schedule Management

B. Requirements Management

C. Configuration Management

D. Growing Your Interpersonal Skills

46. You were just assigned to manage a new project. You were given a Stakeholder Register by your PMO and asked to fill it out. Who would you add to the register?

A. Your Team Members

B. Your Project Sponsor

C. Your Customer

D. Any individual, group, or organization that may affect, be affected by, or perceive themselves to be affected by a decision, activity, or outcome of the project.

47. Your organization is contemplating starting a new project. You have been asked to develop the first draft of a Business Case to state the intended value in the project outcome. You know that a Business Case contains three supporting elements. Which of the following elements would you NOT include in your Business Case?

A.   Business Need

B.   Project Roadmap

C.   Project Justification

D.   Business Strategy

48.   In your role as a Project Manager, you realize that delivering on the vision of the product outweighs creating a specific deliverable. Your team is working on developing a new software application that is intended to bring the business higher productivity. The only deliverable in your project is the completed application. What is a deliverable that could be added to your project to produce the actual desired outcome?

A.   A feature that allows the application to run faster

B.   Improved user interface

C.   Training and coaching

D.   Requirements Traceability Matrix

49.   You are in the final stages of developing a product for your organization. For sure this product will help your organization. But you want to make sure you are adding as much value that you can to the organization as quickly as you possibly can, what is one thing you should do?

A.   Work with organization leaders in advance to ensure project deliverables are put in place as quickly as possible

B.   Go Live with the solution and deliver training

C.   Create an intranet site with information about the solution

D.   Distribute a newsletter containing information about the solution

50.   You are managing a construction project. One of your stakeholders has suggested a change in requirements. This change seems pretty minor, but because you apply 'Systems Thinking', what should you do?

A. Nothing. The change is so minor that no one will care
B. Ignore the suggested change
C. Reject the suggested change
D. Have the stakeholder submit a Change Request and then conduct an impact assessment with the primary contractor and suppliers

Final Project Management Quiz Answers

1. **Project examples could include which of the following?**
A. Publication of a children's book
B. Covid-19 vaccine
C. Human beings landing on the moon
D. All of the above
Answer: D
Rationale: all the options are correct. They are all examples of a project; temporary, unique, and they start and an end.

2. **The *PMBOK® Guide* and the Standard for Project Management are both in one book.**
A. True
B. False
Answer: A
Rationale: this is true. The *PMBOK® Guide* is made up of two parts.

3. **A _____ is a temporary endeavor undertaken to create a unique product, service, or result.**
A. Project
B. Operation
C. Program
D. Portfolio
Answer: A
Rationale: This defines a project.

4. **Fulfillment of project objectives may produce which of the following?**

A. A product that is not unique and can be either a component of another item
B. A non-unique service or a capability to perform a service
C. A unique result, such as an outcome or document
D. A repetitive task to add value to produce a repeat product or service

Answer: C

Rationale: This describes what a project could produce.

5. **Examples of projects include which of the following?**
A. Expanding a tour guide service and merging two organizations
B. Improving a business process within an organization
C. Acquiring a hardware system and exploring for oil in a region
D. All of the options

Answer: D

Rationale: all the options are correct. They are all examples of a project; temporary, unique, and they start and an end.

6. **Projects, programs, subsidiary portfolios, and operations managed as a group to achieve strategic objectives. What does this describe?**
A. Project
B. Operation
C. Program
D. Portfolio

Answer: D

Rationale: this defines a portfolio.

7. **_____ is concerned with the ongoing production of goods and/or services. It ensures that business operations continue efficiently by using the optimal resources needed to meet customer demands.**

A. Project management
B. **Operations management**
C. Program management
D. Portfolio management

Answer: B

Rationale: this defines operations management.

8. **What is a document established by an authority, custom, or general consent as a model or example known as?**
A. **Standard**
B. Regulation
C. Legal Restriction
D. Governmental agency rule

Answer: A

Rationale: this defines a standard.

9. **Which of the following moves an organization from one state to another?**
A. **Project**
B. Process
C. Procedure
D. Benefit

Answer: A

Rationale: the best answer is project.

10. **The benefit that the results of a specific project provide to its stakeholders is known as _____**
A. **Business value**
B. Benefits management
C. Stockholder equity
D. Strategic alignment

Answer: A

Rationale: the best answer is business value.

11. An agile approach to planning____.
A. **Results in plans that encourage change and that are easily changed**
B. Focuses on the plan documents rather than the planning process
C. Results in a fully defined schedule and budget
D. Fully defines product features early in the project

Answer: A

Rationale: Agile results in plans that encourage change and that are easily changed. Agile is a change-based approach – adaptive, not prescriptive

12. Agile is best used when _____
A. There is low variability is needed on the project
B. Change is unlikely and static requirements are needed
C. **Experimentation and discovery are needed for the solution**
D. Little chance of change and high certainty

Answer: C

Rationale: Agile is best used when experimentation and discovery are needed for the solution.

13. Which of the following is most important on all projects?
- *Deliver on Time*
- *Deliver on Budget*
- *Deliver all Planned Scope*
- *Meet Customer Needs*
- *Meet Quality Requirements*
- *Team Satisfaction*

A. Time
B. Budget

C. **The 3 lower-level items on the list**

D. The 3 higher level items on the list

Answer: C

Rationale: the most important elements on all projects revolve around the team, customer and quality. The other elements are not unimportant, but people elements should come first. As the Agile Manifesto states: Individuals and interactions over processes and tools.

14. **Which of these is NOT a function associated with a project?**
    A. Provide oversight and coordination
    B. Present objectives and feedback
    C. **Control the company revenues**
    D. Perform work and contribute insights

Answer: C

Rationale: this is not one of the functions associated with a project.

15. **External environments include:**
    A. Infrastructure
    B. **Academic research**
    C. Information technology software
    D. Resource availability and commercial databases

Answer: B

Rationale: this is not one of the functions associated with a project.

16. **The PMI® Code of Ethics includes _____ (select all that apply)**
    A. **Responsibility and Respect**
    B. Respect and Bureaucracy
    C. Resiliency and Responsibility
    D. **Fairness and Respect**

Answer: A and D

Rationale: the PMI Code of Ethics includes Responsibility, Respect, Fairness and Honesty.

17. The first principle about stewardship includes:

A. Integrity and Rewards

B. Care and Remuneration

C. Trustworthiness and Compliance

D. All of the options

Answer: C

Rationale: the first principle about stewardship includes trustworthiness and compliance.

18. The second principle encourages a _____ team environment.

A. Communicative

B. Collaborative

C. Participative

D. Conniving

Answer: B

Rationale: the second principle encourages a collaborative team environment.

19. Stakeholder engagement is _____ for success

A. A bit important

B. Not important

C. Critical

D. Subjective

Answer: C

Rationale: stakeholder engagement is critical for success.

20. According to PMI, value is _____ and driver of projects.

A. **The ultimate success indicator**

B. The monetary indicator

C. Tangible

D. Quantifiable

Answer: A

Rationale: value is the ultimate success indicator.

21. According to PMI:

A. **A project is a system**

B. Systems occasionally change

C. A project is not a system

D. Systems thinking is a partial view

Answer: A

Rationale: A project is a system.

22. Which of these terms best describes leadership?

A. Authority

B. Position

C. Title

D. **Influence**

Answer: D

Rationale: the true measure of leadership is influence (John C. Maxwell). Although one's position, title and authority are a starting point for any leader, the word the best sums it up is influence.

23. According to PMI, tailoring is _____

A. Iterative

B. Continuous

C. A constant process

D. **All of the above**

Answer: D

Rationale: all the options describe the nature of tailoring.

24. According to PMI, quality involves _____

A. Aggravating stakeholders
B. Meeting acceptance criteria
C. Ensuring project processes are inappropriate
D. All of the options

Answer: B

Rationale: the best option is meeting acceptance criteria.

25. According to PMI, complexity is the result of _____

A. Human behavior
B. System interactions
C. Uncertainty and ambiguity
D. All of the options

Answer: D

Rationale: all the options are correct. Complexity is the result of all 3 options.

26. Project risk management should be _____
A. Appropriate to the significance of the risk
B. Cost effective in meeting personal goals and targets
C. Realistic within the operations context
D. Disagreed upon by all parties

Answer: A

Rationale: the best option is "appropriate to the significance of the risk". The question is about projects not operations or personal goals.

27. Resiliency is best described as the _____
A. Ability to respond to change
B. Ability to absorb impacts/recover
C. Ability to configure a project
D. Ability to focus on project outcomes

Answer: B

Rationale: this is the best description of resiliency. Ability to absorb impacts/recover.

28. According to PMI, too much change _____

A. Could lead to over-energizing the team

B. Could lead to change fatigue and resistance

C. Could help enable stakeholder engagement

D. Is not possible because change always contributes

Answer: B

Rationale: the best option is "too much change could lead to change fatigue and resistance."

29. You are working on a project with low requirements uncertainty and a low technical uncertainty. Due to these low levels of uncertainty, which model should you select?

A. Hybrid

B. Agile

C. Iterative

D. Predictive

Answer: D

Rationale: based on the Stacey Complexity Model, the best option is Predictive.

30. Which of the following factors typically does not influence the nature of project delivery method selected?

A. Deliverable

B. Organization

C. Project

D. Motivation and machines

Answer: D

Rationale: motivation and machines does not influence of project delivery method selected.

31. Which of the following is not typically a life-cycle phase?

A. Feasibility, Design

B. Build, Test

C. Deploy, Close

D. Monitoring and Controlling

Answer: D

Rationale: Monitoring and Controlling are process groups not life-cycle phases.

32. Metrics on a project should not be planned until the executing stage.

A. True

B. False

Answer: B

Rationale: False. Metrics should be planned into the project.

33. Values clustered around a desired value with little scatter. What does this describe?

A. Highly Accurate and Highly Precise

B. Accuracy is low

C. Precision is high

D. Defective

Answer: A

Rationale: this describes high accuracy and high precision.

34. In agile, the Scrum Master is solely accountable for ensuring project process conferment.

A. True

B. False

Answer: B

Rationale: this is the responsibility of the team.

35. The best approach for delivery in Kanban is:

A. Every 2 weeks

B. Every 4 weeks

C. When it makes sense to do so

D. At the specific order of the flow master

Answer: C

Rationale: when it makes sense to do so

36. Which of the following is NOT a legit artifact of agile?

A. Burn up chart

B. Burn down chart

C. Risk baseline

D. Sprint backlog

Answer: C

Rationale: Risk baseline is not a legit artifact of agile. The others are.

37. Which of the following is NOT a risk?

A. Resource X has been called off the project

B. Resource Y may not be available

C. Resource Z a key resource may be called off the project

D. The build has a reputation for being unstable

Answer: A

Rationale: This option is the one thing that is certain! It is an ISSUE! Everything else is uncertain (which describes a risk! Uncertain events that could impact the project).

38. You are managing a project. One of your team members has an opportunity to move onto another project that would be an incredible opportunity for them. Your project is critical and you know with one phone call, you could prevent this person from leaving your team. What should you do?

A. Do nothing

B. Make the call so as not to lose this valuable resource

C. Support your team member's access to opportunity

D. Offer up another team member that is not as valuable to your team

Answer: C

Rationale: Principle 1 - Be a diligent, respectful, and caring steward.
The right thing to do in accordance with principle one is to enable
information to flow to those who are privy to it.

39. **You are managing a construction project. You have received
    quotes from three different suppliers and are currently
    evaluating the proposals. After work one evening, you just
    happened to bump into one of the suppliers at your favorite
    hang-out. After a few minutes of casual conversation, he
    makes the statement that if his company is chosen as the
    supplier that he will personally see that you get financially
    compensated. What should you do?**

A. Ask how much you would be compensated
B. **Politely excuse yourself from this conversation because
   stewards behave honestly and ethically**
C. Take him up on the offer because no one will ever know
D. Postpone your answer until you talk with your lawyer friend

Answer: B

Rationale: Principle 1 - Be a diligent, respectful, and caring steward.
The right thing to do in accordance with the PMI code of ethics is to
recuse yourself from this conversation.

40. **You become aware that the FAA is planning to change the
    flight paths for a major airport located just two miles from
    your nuclear plant. The new fight path would reduce airline
    noise for local residents but would require more than 50% of
    the air traffic to fly directly over the cooling towers. What
    should you do?**

A. **Seek appropriate counsel and guidance**
B. Do nothing
C. Support the FAA plans for change
D. Contact the FAA and partition for the change not to occur

Answer: A

Rationale: Principle 1 - Be a diligent, respectful, and caring steward. The best course of action is to seek appropriate counsel and guidance. Not doing anything is not being proactive. This is not in the spirit of principle number one.

41. **You have just been assigned to a new project. Both you as well as all of your team members are very experienced but have never worked together on the same project before. What is the first thing you should do?**

A. Create a Project Charter
B. Document the requirements for the project
C. Pick a suitable collaboration software for your team
D. Develop a Team Agreement

Answer: D

Rationale: since you have been assigned to this new project, you could infer that you have been named the project manager as documented in a project charter. The situation being described alludes to a key step in teamwork which is to develop the team agreement which is also known as a social contract or team contract.

42. **You have been assigned to manage a project with many team members. You know that an organizational structure will help coordinate the effort associated with the project work. You know these structures can be based upon a number of factors. You want to develop an organization structure for your project, which of the following is NOT an approach you could use?**

A. By Role
B. By Function
C. By Experience
D. By Authority

Answer: C

Rationale: Principle 2 - Create a collaborative team environment. Organizations are not structured by experience. All the other options are correct.

43. **You know that a diverse project team can enrich the project environment by bringing together different perspectives. You are at a point in the project where you need to bring on additional resources. Your current team is comprised of organizational staff. Since you are wanting to bring in a fresh perspective, which option would you not choose to bring on?**

A. Contracted Contributors

B. Organizational Staff

C. Volunteers

D. External Third Parties

Answer: B

Rationale: the question asks for an option to not choose. Pay close attention to the word not as you answer exam questions. You would bring on all the other options except organizational stuff because these will not give you a fresh perspective.

44. **Engaging with stakeholders is time-intensive during project planning. The sponsor would like to know what all the fuss is about and get an explanation from you as the project manager about what is taking so long. How would you explain the why the time is needed?**

A. **To effectively engage stakeholders in project decisions and execution based on the analysis of their needs, interests, and potential impact**

B. To ensure the stakeholders are receiving the reports in the format they would like

C. To effectively place the right people in the correct role to support achieving the project objectives on time and within budget

D. To be able to document which stakeholder is unaware, neutral, leading, or supportive

Answer: A

Rationale: Principle 3 - Effectively engage with stakeholders. The best and most conclusive option is based on effective engagement.

Effective engagement spans across the entire project and it does take time.

45. **You are relatively new to Project Management. You want to do a little research or studying of the topic Stakeholder Engagement. Which course should you take?**
A. Schedule Management
B. Requirements Management
C. Configuration Management
D. **Growing Your Interpersonal Skills**

Answer: D

Rationale: Principle 3 - Effectively engage with stakeholders. The most appropriate answer is growing your interpersonal skills. Effective stakeholder engagement requires impeccable interpersonal skills..

46. **You were just assigned to manage a new project. You were given a Stakeholder Register by your PMO and asked to fill it out. Who would you add to the register?**
A. Your Team Members
B. Your Project Sponsor
C. Your Customer
D. **Any individual, group, or organization that may affect, be affected by, or perceive themselves to be affected by a decision, activity, or outcome of the project.**

Answer: D

Rationale: this is the best option to choose because it describes who stakeholders are. Not only could stakeholders be the project sponsor and customer but also team members as well as anyone else who could affect the project or may be affected by the project or perceive to be affected by the project.

47. **Your organization is contemplating starting a new project. You have been asked to develop the first draft of a Business Case to state the intended value in the project outcome. You**

know that a Business Case contains three supporting elements. Which of the following elements would you NOT include in your Business Case?

A. Business Need
B. **Project Roadmap**
C. Project Justification
D. Business Strategy

Answer: B

Rationale: the best option is the project road map because this is not typically included in a business case. Recall that the business case is prepared before the project is authorized. The product roadmap will typically be developed later on in the process after project authorization.

48. **In your role as a Project Manager, you realize that delivering on the vision of the product outweighs creating a specific deliverable. Your team is working on developing a new software application that is intended to bring the business higher productivity. The only deliverable in your project is the completed application. What is a deliverable that could be added to your project to produce the actual desired outcome?**

A. A feature that allows the application to run faster
B. Improved user interface
C. **Training and coaching**
D. Requirements Traceability Matrix

Answer: C

Rationale: the best option is training and coaching because this is focused on outcomes as opposed to output.

49. **You are in the final stages of developing a product for your organization. For sure this product will help your organization. But you want to make sure you are adding as much value that you can to the organization as quickly as you possibly can, what is one thing you should do?**

A. **Work with organization leaders in advance to ensure project deliverables are put in place as quickly as possible**
B. Go Live with the solution and deliver training
C. Create an intranet site with information about the solution
D. Distribute a newsletter containing information about the solution

Answer: A

Rationale: The best answer is focused on ensuring deliverables are put in place as quickly as possible. The option regarding going live and then delivering training is not wise. People should be trained first before going live. The other options do not add relevant value early to the customer. Some of these options are focused on documentation as opposed to a working product.

50. **You are managing a construction project. One of your stakeholders has suggested a change in requirements. This change seems pretty minor, but because you apply 'Systems Thinking', what should you do?**
A. Nothing. The change is so minor that no one will care
B. Ignore the suggested change
C. Reject the suggested change
D. **Have the stakeholder submit a Change Request and then conduct an impact assessment with the primary contractor and suppliers**

Answer: D

Rationale: a change request should be submitted. Systems thinking requires looking at the big picture view of a situation and considering what a change could do to the entire system. Remember Principle 5 - Recognize, evaluate, and respond to system interactions.

About the Author

Phill C. Akinwale, PMP has managed operational endeavors, projects and project controls across government and private sectors in various companies, including Motorola, Honeywell, Emerson, Skillsoft, Citigroup, Iron Mountain, Brown and Caldwell, US Airways and CVS Caremark. With his extensive experience in various facets of Project Management and rigorous project controls, he has trained project management worldwide (NASA, FBI, USAF, USACE, US Army, Department of Transport) across five PMBOK® Guide editions over the last 15 years.

He holds eight project management certifications with five in Agile Project Management (CSM, PMI-ACP, PSM, PSPO, PAL). As a John Maxwell Certified Coach and Speaker, Phill delivers workshops, seminars, keynote speaking, and coaching in leadership and soft skills. Working together with you and your team or organization, he will guide you in the desired direction and equip you to reach your goals. Books he has authored include: The No-Good Leader, Earned Value Basics and Project Management Mid-Level to C-Level.

www.praizion.com

Thanks for reading! Please add a short review on Amazon and let me know what you thought!

Watch the *PMBOK® Guide* Seventh Edition Training Video from Praizion:

https://projectmanagementdoctor.com/pmbokguide7-training

Thanks and best wishes!

Phill Akinwale, PMP, OPM3, ACP